The Truth He Brought
William S. Crowdy
A Prophet of God

Bible quotations are from the King James Version

Printed on acid-free paper.

Copyright © 2021 Sharon E. Jones Roberts
Majestic International Books
Chesapeake, VA

ISBN 978-0-578-96430-0
All rights reserved. No part of this publication may be reproduced, stored in a retrieval system, or transmitted in any form or by any means, electronic, mechanical, recording or otherwise, without the prior written permission of the author.

Majestic International Books.com

This work is dedicated with gratitude, humility and love to an adorer of education, a lover of learning and teaching, a kind and caring man of God.

Rabbi Levi Solomon Plummer

His Predecessors

Prophet William S. Crowdy

Chief Joseph W. Crowdy

Bishop William H. Plummer

Counselor Calvin S. Skinner

Rabbi Howard Z. Plummer

His Immediate Successors

Rabbi Jehu A. Crowdy, Jr.

Rabbi Phillip E. McNeil

His Contemporary

Rabbi Jehu A. Crowdy, Sr.

Prophet William S. Crowdy

Preface

I give thanks and praise to God for the privilege of preparing and presenting this work. I also am thankful for the inspiration I received from St. Gertrude Hudson's composition, "Always Remember God's Prophet, William S. Crowdy." As a fourth generation member of Church of God and Saints of Christ, Temple Beth El, Suffolk, VA, International Headquarters, I acknowledge and thank God for my relatives who are responsible for me being a member of this religious community. I assure you that my affection for my faith community does not imply a lack of respect or appreciation for other faith communities. I genuinely believe that the reality that some call God does not have a religion any more than a gender or a race. Our various religious traditions merely represent our human attempt to know, understand and be in relationship with that which we believe to be and to care about our earthly existence. I also acknowledge and give thanks for many of the teachers and professors that I have benefited from over the years, including the Religious Educator Elder Franklin H. Benson. I am especially thankful to Nicole Morgan-Clark for reading drafts of this work and providing invaluable professional feedback. Finally, the information contained in this publication reflects my personal views and not the official position of Church of God and Saints of Christ, Temple Beth El, Suffolk, VA, International Headquarters. To learn about its official position on its history and doctrine, visit the website: www.cogasoc.org

"Wherefore by their fruits ye shall know them."

Introduction

"Before I formed thee in the belly I knew thee; and before thou camest forth out of the womb I sanctified thee, and I ordained thee a prophet unto the nations." Jeremiah 1:5

William Saunders Crowdy was born a slave on August 11, 1847 at Charlotte Hall, St. Mary's County, Maryland. When he was sixteen, he ran away, joined the Union Army, serving from 1863 until 1866. After the Civil War, he continued military service from 1867 to 1872. Eventually, he relocated to Kansas City, Missouri, where he married, fathered three children: a daughter and two sons, and worked as a cook, as his mother had done at the Charlotte Hall plantation.[1] In September of 1891, he acquired 160 acres near Guthrie, Oklahoma under the Federal Homestead Settlement program. He continued to work as a cook while farming his land, and participating in his community as a deacon in a Baptist church, captain of a black militia, and member of the Masons.[2]

This was his life, when in the spring of 1893, while working on his farm, he had the prophetic vision that culminated in the creation of the Church of God and

Saints of Christ. [3] In his Vision, he was shown seven keys. Each key contained a statement and biblical reference. The first key was inscribed Church of God and Saints of Christ. The biblical reference was I Corinthians chapter one verse two. Rabbi Levi S. Plummer, the sixth executive leader of the Congregation, gave an interpretation for each of the seven keys. The interpretation for the first key is Divine ownership. In his Vision, Prophet Crowdy also was shown a Bible and told to eat it up. He immediately began preaching on the streets in Guthrie and neighboring towns. When he preached, he quoted the Bible by chapter and verse. One of his biographers says of this new characteristic:

> He himself could not believe that he actually knew the Bible but would come home and look for some of the things that he had quoted as being in such and such a chapter of the Bible to see if they were there. It was always amazing to him that he found them, every word, just as he had said. [4]

Prophet Crowdy subsequently incorporated the organization in 1896 in Emporia, Kansas. He continued to travel from city to city preaching his revelation until his death on August 4, 1908.

During those early years, local tabernacles were established around the United States, Canada and South Africa. In fact, in 1898, there were twenty-eight tabernacles in the state of Kansas alone. [5] The arrival of the organization in Africa was itself a clear demonstration of Prophet Crowdy's prophetic legitimacy.

The work in Africa was started by Bishop Albert Christian. In 1902, he was working as a missionary in Africa when he began dreaming repeatedly of a man he did not know. In response to his dreams, he left Africa and went to England and then the United States where he traveled first to New York City and then Philadelphia. As he was walking along Philadelphia's Fitzwater street, he saw the man from his dreams. It was Prophet Crowdy. According to the *Re-Establishing Years,* Prophet Crowdy told Albert Christian that he was the person the Lord wanted to take the gospel of the

Church of God and Saints of Christ to Africa. Albert Christian remained with Prophet Crowdy until 1903. Prophet Crowdy made him an Elder, an Evangelist and finally a Bishop before sending him to Cape Colony, South Africa as his representative. [6]

The purchase of forty acres in what is now Suffolk, Virginia in July of 1903 is additional verification of Prophet Crowdy's prophetic authenticity. Prophet Crowdy was walking in the area when he was approached by a man who asked him if he wanted to buy some land. Initially, he said no, but as he took five steps, he said, God told him to buy it for the saints. [7] Individual members donated three dollars each to facilitate the purchase. [8] That acreage remains part of the Congregation's property at its International Headquarters in Suffolk. [9] In 1909, the Congregation lost those first forty acres. Miraculously, Mr. John Eberwine, a white farmer who purchased the property at auction, refused to sell it to anyone other than the Church. On September 13, 1920, Bishop William H. Plummer, the third executive leader, with the financial support of the membership repurchased the property. [10] Bishop William H. Plummer not only redeemed the initial forty acres, but over the next four years he purchased hundreds of additional acreage. [11] All of this land acquisition occurring in a southern state during the era of Jim Crow and racial segregation.

In 1893, Prophet Crowdy undoubtedly was enjoying his life as a husband and father, community leader and farmer when the Spirit of God corralled him in such a way that transformed his being, his life and his legacy. Before he died, he told his members that he had given them the religion of the Congregation "in chunks, but there were men coming behind him who would break it up into pieces." This proclamation placed the Church of God and Saints of Christ upon a sound foundation. One undergirded by a process of theological and organizational refinement that has allowed it to continuously evolve in accordance with the Vision God gave to his prophet William S. Crowdy. Consequently, no single writing can fully describe or explain the way of life corporately identified as Church of God and Saints of Christ, Temple Beth El, Suffolk, VA, International Headquarters. *The Truth He Brought,* merely endeavors to discuss portions of three facets of Prophet Crowdy's work: inter-racial worship and the racial identity of the biblical Israelites and Jesus; the truth that women can preach and pastor; and some distinctive features of the religious community he established based on the prophetic tradition of the Hebrew Bible and the New Testament scriptures.

Race

"...he giveth to all life, and breath, and all things; And hath made of one blood all nations of men for to dwell on all the face of the earth." Acts 17:25- 26

Prophet Crowdy's views about race in society and biblical history denote the truth and universality of his revelation. He called himself "the World's Evangelist" the title shown to him in his Vision. As he embarked upon his mission, he modeled racial inclusion and equality in the numerous towns where he preached in Kansas and other western states. [12] James M. Grove, a white grocery store owner, joined Prophet Crowdy in Topeka, Kansas. Prophet Crowdy ordained him an Elder, appointed him to the Congregation's first Presbytery Board, and made him the first Bishop in the organization. [13] Prophet Crowdy's successor, Chief Joseph W. Crowdy, gave Bishop Grove the honor of delivering the eulogy at Prophet Crowdy's funeral in Newark, New Jersey. [14] The Chief also allowed Bishop Grove to retain his position as Bishop of the West. When a split occurred in the Congregation in 1908, the western tabernacles stayed with Bishop Grove. [15]

Bishop Grove was not the only white minister who served under Prophet Crowdy's leadership. In fact most of the officers and members in the west were white. [16] 1896, the year the Church of God and Saints of Christ was founded, was the same year the Supreme Court issued its infamous *Plessy v. Ferguson* decision. The case introduced the principle, "separate but equal," by upholding the South's racial segregation laws and implicitly legitimizing racial segregation practices nationwide. The fact that Prophet Crowdy attracted white members at a time when racial segregation was the rule in every aspect of American society, reflected racial impartiality and equality, and affirmed his commission as, "a prophet of God sent to the whole world."

Church of God and Saints of Christ was not the only religious organization to embrace inter-racial membership during the period of segregation. [17] Still, inter-racial worship in the United States then and now remains the exception. A November 2020 Washington Post story found an increase in inter-racial congregations from 6% to 16% during the opening decades of the twenty first century. The reporter found that this modest increase in inter-racial worship occurred because blacks joined majority white congregations or started their own inter-racial ones, with few whites joining predominately black churches. [18] It is true that Church of God and Saints of Christ, Temple Beth El, Suffolk, VA, International Headquarters is primarily an African American and black African congregation. It also is true that people of any race always have been welcomed to become members.

Prophet Crowdy's foresight on the issue of race also can been seen in his preaching that the biblical Israelites and Jesus were black. [19] He did so decades before universal awareness of the African origin of human civilization, and when some scholars were alleging that the ancient Egyptians and other ancient biblical civilizations were white. For example, from Charles Copher's article, "The Black Presence in the Old Testament," "All known ancient races in the region [the biblical world] which concerns us here belonged to the so-called "white" or "Caucasian" race, with the exception of the Cushite ("Ethiopians") who were strongly Negroid in type, as we know from many

Egyptian paintings."[20] As the twentieth century unfolded, scholars began to corroborate Prophet Crowdy's insight on this subject.

One such scholar was Cain Hope Felder. In his essay *Race, Racism, and the Biblical Narratives,* he states:

> The specific racial type of the Biblical Hebrews is itself quite difficult to determine. Scholars today generally recognize that the Biblical Hebrews probably emerged as an amalgamation of races rather than from any pure stock. When they departed from Egypt, they may well have been Afro-Asiatics – scarcely were any "Europeans part of the "mixed multitude."[21]

In his essay *Reading Race, Reading the Bible,* Peter Nash embraces the term Afro- Asiatic and expressly states, "...the people who populated the Old Testament were people of color, or Black to be more specific..."[22] These descriptions of the biblical Hebrews as Afro-Asiatics is somewhat perplexing since we tend to associate Asia with China, Japan, and other Pacific Asian countries. A Google search instantly reminds us that Asia is the world's largest continent, and the region, that since 1902 has been called the Middle East, is located in its southwest sector. Scholars of the ancient world refer to this area as the Ancient Near East. It consists of Mesopotamia, modern Iraq, Syria, Turkey, Lebanon, Israel, Palestine, and Iran. [23] Some scholars include Egypt among the countries of the Ancient Near East, although Egypt is in Africa not Asia. Nevertheless, because of Egypt's and other ancient African countries' impact on the history of the Ancient Near East, it is appropriate to include it in any discussion of the area.

Notwithstanding the abundance of information that the modern world has acquired about Egypt, the oldest known civilization in the Ancient Near East is the Sumerians of Mesopotamia. Knowledge of the Sumerians was discovered accidentally as archaeologists were searching for remnants of the Babylonians and Assyrians. As one writer exclaimed:

> "They did indeed find the Babylonians; but they also found the monuments and documents of a people hitherto unknown, a people who preceded the Babylonians and Assyrians, and who had created the most ancient of the

historical cultures known, that of the Sumerians."[24]

In his discussion of the Sumerians, John Jackson said:

> The ancient inhabitants of Mesopotamia are sometimes called the Chaldeans, but they were latecomers to the area. Preceding them were the Sumerians, Akkadians, Babylonians, and Assyrians. The earliest civilization was that of the Sumerians. They are described in the Asssyrio - Babylonian inscriptions as a black-faced people...[25]

Jackson also explained that at one time all of the people of Sudan, Egypt, Arabia, Palestine, Western Asia and India were considered Ethiopians. He quotes an historian of the history of Ethiopia:

> It seems certain that classical historians and geographers called the region from India to Egypt, both countries inclusive, by the name of Ethiopia, and in consequence they regarded all the dark skinned and black people who inhabited it as Ethiopians. Mention is made of Eastern and Western Ethiopians, and it is

> probable that the Eastern were Asiatics and the Western Africans. [26]

This reference indicates that those referred to as Eastern or Western, Asiatics or Africans, were both considered Ethiopians – dark skinned and black people.

Charles Copher offered additional corroboration of Prophet Crowdy's racial declarations about the biblical Israelites when he wrote:

> According to one tradition (Gen. 11:31; Neh. 9:7; Acts 7:2- 4) the original home of Abraham was Ur of the Chaldeans – a land whose earliest inhabitants included blacks. Representative of the black presence were the Sumerians, who referred to themselves as the "black-headed ones," indicative of skin color rather than of mere color of the hairs, as some would argue. [27]

Copher agreed with the conclusion that the original Hebrews were a racially mixed people. The ancestral roots of those racially mixed Hebrews who became the biblical Israelites were irrefutably black not white, African and not European. Specifically, their racial roots were the ancient Ethiopians. Keeping in mind that ancient Ethiopia geographically was significantly more expansive than the country that is Ethiopia today and gave birth to the ancient civilizations of Sumer and Egypt.

Cain Hope Felder's work equally supports Prophet Crowdy's teaching about the biblical Jesus. In the introduction to *The Original African Heritage Study Bible* he states:

> We can now return to the question of the race of Jesus of Nazareth. His mother, Mary, was Afro-Asiatic and probably looked like a typical Yemenite, Trinidadian, or African American of today...Mary, Joseph and Jesus were neither Greek nor Roman. With the marvelous oils and watercolors of the painter's brush, the world gradually witnessed the rebirth of Jesus, as medieval and Renaissance artists made him suitable for the portrayal of Christianity as a "European religion. Thus there developed a brand new manger scene, with the infant Jesus and his parents reimaged. Ancient darker, and

> clearly more African, icons were discarded or destroyed. [28]

The editors conclude their explication by addressing general skepticism toward their contention:

> Many in the 1990s who think of a black Jesus as an oddity or scandalous distortion of historical facts insist that Jesus was Semitic, or Middle Eastern. However, to call Jesus Semitic does not take us very far, because this nineteenth-century term refers not to a racial type, but to a family of languages including both Hebrew and Ethiopic. About the same time that the European academy coined the term *Semitic,* it also created the geographical designation called the Middle East – all in an effort to avoid talking about Africa! [29]

In 2021, there still may be many who are unaware that the biblical Israelites and Jesus, in today's language, were people of color. Prophet Crowdy preached this truth at the dawn of the twentieth century, and since then modern scholarship has confirmed the truth that he preached.

Prophet Crowdy's Women Elders

"So God created man in his own image, in the image of God created he him; male and female created he them." Genesis 1:27

One might expect that since Prophet Crowdy readily embraced inter-racial membership, he also fully endorsed ministerial gender equality. The issue of women preachers, please note preachers, in Church of God and Saints of Christ like that concerning women preachers in most religious organizations in the nineteenth and early twentieth centuries is complex. For example, the 1889 story of a Jewish woman in Philadelphia posing the question through her fictional character Dora, "Could not our women be ministers?" [30] At first glance, one could argue that from November 1896 until April 1906, Prophet Crowdy did practice ministerial gender equality. During that period, the Sister Elders, or women Elders, as Prophet Crowdy called them, sat on the pulpit with the male Elders. Like the men, the women were called "Elder Jones" not "Sister Elder Jones" as they are today. Yet, a closer look compels the conclusion that this was not gender ministerial equality. Fortunately, Prophet Crowdy's first biographer was a woman, his eldest granddaughter, Beersheba Crowdy Walker Granison.

St. Beersheba was a teacher who taught in the public schools in Philadelphia. Later, while raising her six children, she received a Bachelor of Science from the University of Pennsylvania and Master of Science from Temple University. For much of the lifetime of her first husband, Elder John Prince Walker, Sr., they traveled to different cities to collect photographs and interview older members of the Congregation. Together, they devoted innumerable hours researching, compiling, and preserving that history. The little that we know about Prophet Crowdy's women Elders is because of their book, *Life and Works of William Saunders Crowdy,* which documented the women Elders' presence and some of their activities:

> not only men were used as pastors; some of the Prophet's best workers were women. A large church was established in Utica and left in care of Sister Elder Lavender, a former slave who had come north before Emancipation on the Underground Railway. She joined the church in

> Utica and was ordained by the Prophet and left in charge. .[31]

In comments concerning the 1902 Annual Assembly (the Congregation's national business conclave) which took place in Philadelphia, St. Beersheba noted: "Female Elders sat on the pulpit at this time, and one of them, Elder Mary Certain (Late U.S. Grand Exhorter) led the congregation in prayer."[32] There was also Elder Huldah Wells of Jersey City, NJ who is included in the list of tabernacles with their respective pastors reporting to the 1904 Annual Assembly.[33] Foremost though among these women Elders was Evangelist Malinda Morris who became the first female Evangelist in the Congregation.[34]

Malinda Morris was born in 1867 in Danville, Virginia. When she and her husband moved to New York City in 1899, she was a Baptist Missionary and dedicated member of the Order of Eastern Stars. In New York, she heard the preaching of Prophet William S. Crowdy and joined the Church of God and Saints of Christ. She was made a Sister Elder at the Annual Assembly in Philadelphia in 1900 or 1901.[35] In excerpts from the minutes of the 1902 Assembly, Elder Malinda Morris is listed as one of the two pastors of the Newark Tabernacle, and as delivering the sermon at one of the sessions. [36] She also is recorded as one of the Newark pastors in excerpts from the 1904 minutes. [37] She still is identified as Elder Malinda Morris in a statement St. Beersheba relates from one of Prophet Crowdy's epistles: "...women pastors there is none but one – that is Elder Malinda Morris – the other Elders are over the Daughters of Jerusalem and Sisters of Mercy." [38]

At the 1906 Passover in Plainfield, New Jersey, Prophet Crowdy removed the women Elders from the pulpit. Regarding that event, we' re told: "Of them all, Evangelist Malinda Morris seemed to take it the hardest; it is said that she alone cried. At a later time, the Prophet allowed her to resume her seat on the rostrum." [39] In two 1908 writings about Prophet William S. Crowdy, Evangelist Morris is referred to as Chief Evangelist Malinda D. Morris as well as the pastor of the Newark, New Jersey Tabernacle. [40] As previously mentioned, Prophet Crowdy was in Newark when he died on August 4, 1908. It was at the home of Evangelist

Malinda Morris that he laid for public viewing prior to his burial. [41]

After Prophet William S. Crowdy passed, Evangelist Morris was the subject of a lawsuit to remove her as pastor of the Newark Tabernacle. According to her organization's oral history, she was inspired to use the word "Independent" in the court proceedings. When the court awarded her the Newark Tabernacle, she started her own church and named it Independent Church of God and Saints of Christ.

Evangelist Malinda Morris died in 1937. At her request, her eulogy was delivered by Rabbi Howard Z. Plummer, the fifth executive leader of Church of God and Saints of Christ. His subject was, "The Works of Dorcas;" possibly from Acts 9:36: "Now there was at Joppa a certain disciple named Tabitha, which by interpretation is called Dorcas: this woman was full of good works and alms deeds which she did." The seventh executive leader, Rabbi Jehu A. Crowdy, Jr., paid tribute to Evangelist Morris when he told his Congregation that she was one of two individuals who stuck with Prophet William S. Crowdy. Evangelist Morris' members called her Queen Malinda Morris. The church she started still exists in Newark, and fifth generation of its members speak of her life and ministry with profound admiration. In 2014, the city of Newark renamed the street where their present edifice is located: Queen Malinda Dora Morris Way.

The information concerning the women Elders raises several questions. First, why did Prophet Crowdy remove the Sister Elders from the pulpit after affording them that honor for the first ten years of the organization. Of course, there are numerous personal opinions about why this happened; the most obvious being God told him to do it, even though there is no known record of any statement by Prophet Crowdy that explicitly reveals that as the reason for his decision. As we saw with the purchase of the forty acres, Prophet William S. Crowdy was not the least bit reluctant to share the impetus for actions he took. This includes his decision to formally organize his work.

Initially, Prophet Crowdy's custom was to visit a town or city, preach, baptize and wash the feet of converts, appoint one as the Elder in charge, and then move on to another location. [42] That changed slightly after an encounter he had with a man in Chicago which St. Beersheba meticulously recounts:

> Most of his preaching in Chicago was on State Street and one evening as he was preaching there, an Irishman, drunk, stopped to listen. When the sermon was about over, police came to stop him. The Irishman said to him, "old man, there is no mistake that you have the gospel, and if you were organized, they wouldn't arrest you so much." The Prophet said he stopped and listened attentively, the Irishman went on to ask, "have you any members?" "Yes," said the Prophet. "I have several hundred members that I have baptized altogether here and west of here." "Well," said the Irishman, "go back and get some of your people to ordain you a Bishop, and organize yourself, then you won't be arrested so much." The Prophet said he looked at the man who had given him this counsel. The Irishman was so drunk that he couldn't stand straight, but not so drunk that he couldn't give him advice. He said he realized that the man was telling him

> the truth, he thanked him, and as he went away with the police, he began to plan what to do. As soon as he was released this time, he went to the home of a member, told of the incident with the man on the street, and began to lay plans for his first general gathering so that he could be ordained in the sight of all the people. [43]

Prophet Crowdy, who had been arrested over twenty times, freely shared with his members that he received the idea to formally organize the organization from that conversation with the Irishman. In addition, when a member questioned him about his edict that members go back to their first husbands and wives, he replied, "This is the Lord God speaking to us all." [44] Therefore, if the decision to remove the women Elders from the pulpit was motivated by a Divine mandate, it appears to have been in the nature and character of Prophet Crowdy to say so. Moreover, he did allow Evangelist Malinda Morris to return to sitting on the pulpit.

Given the times in which these women Elders lived, we can surmise that sexism played a role in their plight. The word sexism was not used until the 1960s.[45] The belief that women were inferior to men, however, and appropriately subordinate members of society is ancient. The practice of discriminating against women is based on the ancient Greco- Roman culture's attitudes about women's place in society and their substandard intellectual abilities. This mindset infiltrated Western religion and became a fundamental feature of Western Civilization. In her research, Bettye Collier- Thomas discovered a statement in the minutes of an 1890 black denomination's Minister Conference which she correctly concluded captured the sexist views about women in the church and society at large. "Is woman inferior to man?" The chairman of the meetings stated, "Sad as it may be, woman is as inferior to man as man is to God." [46]

There are two additional facts that are relevant to the predicament of the women Elders. In 1903, the Sister Elders were given a different uniform from the other female members. [47] The differentiation was reflected in Prophet Crowdy's 1906 announcement concerning the attire for that upcoming Passover. [48] Thus after 1903, the women Elders were sitting on the pulpit with the men and dressed in a way that visibly distinguished them from the other women in the congregation. Additionally, excerpts from the minutes of the 1904 Assembly reference a law prohibiting women from sitting on the pulpit. [49] This fact most likely is derived from the minutes of the Board of Presbytery, the lawmaking body of the Congregation, that for over one hundred years was comprised exclusively of male ministers. (It must be acknowledged that in 2019 the Board of Presbytery received its first female member and in 2021 three of its thirteen members were women.) So, at least two years before the women Elders were removed from the pulpit, there is evidence of formal opposition to their status by the Board of Presbytery which at that time was comprised of all male Elders

The second question that arises from this history of the women Elders is despite their initial elevated seating position were these women ministers? It is often said that every church member has a ministry, but that does not mean that in the performance of their ministry, every member is a minister. The women Elders, like the present Sister Elders, were preachers. Yet, just as every minister is not a pastor, every preacher is not an ordained or even licensed minister. Collier- Thomas offers the following definition of ordination in her study of black women preachers:

> Ordination is the process by which a preacher's ministry is officially legitimated by a religious tradition. It is a credentialing process that enables one to participate fully in a tradition, to acquire certain rights, and to assume certain responsibilities denied to an unordained minister. It provides authorization for a minister to pastor a church and to ascend to other positions in a religious organization's hierarchy. [50]

It is obvious from several statements Prophet Crowdy made that there were two groups of women Elders: those who were pastors of tabernacles and those who were exhorters for the Daughters of Jerusalem and Sisters of Mercy, the women's auxiliary of Church of God and Saints of Christ. First there is the statement mentioned earlier, "...women pastors there is none but one – that is Elder Malinda Morris – the other Elders are over the Daughters of Jerusalem and Sisters of Mercy." [51] In an epistle in which he directly addressed the women Elders he said, "any women elder who is only an exhorter…"[52] In his epistle entitled, "*Ministers Seeking Honor Too Soon,*" he wrote, "a man or woman who is holding a congregation…"[53] Admittedly, most of the women Elders were not pastors but exhorters. It does not appear that the exhorters were ministers, even when they were seated on the pulpit. It is unclear whether this also applies to the women Elders who were pastors.

With respect to St. Beersheba's account that Sister Elder Lavender was ordained by Prophet Crowdy. Not all ministers participate in a formal ordination ceremony. Some, at least in Church of God and Saints of Christ, are just appointed and licensed as Elders, and there is no noticeable distinction between the ministers who participate in a formal ordination ceremony and those who do not. It is possible that St. Beersheba viewed and hence used the terms appointed and ordained as it related to Elders interchangeably. We cannot definitively know whether Prophet Crowdy gave Sister Elder Lavender a formal ordination or whether he just appointed her the Elder-in- Charge of the Utica Tabernacle. Nor do we know whether Prophet Crowdy considered her and the other women pastors ministers equivalent to the men. In any event, by 1908, there was only one, Evangelist Malinda Morris, still seated on the pulpit. Perhaps that is the reason the effort was made to remove her as the pastor of the Newark Tabernacle.

Well into the twentieth century, many religious communities still were debating whether it was proper for women to preach, let alone pastor a congregation. Prophet William S. Crowdy showed that women could preach and pastor. Although his women Elders did not have genuine ministerial equality, the lingering presence of Evangelist Malinda Morris on the pulpit and as pastor of the Newark Tabernacle may have signaled that such equality was possible, even inevitable. (On March 31, 2021 during the virtual Passover, Chief Rabbi Phillip E. McNeil announced that the cultural bias of gender inequality was not of God, and that the Church of God and Saints of Christ was going to have female ministers. The first female ministers were appointed in July, 2021 during the virtual Annual Assembly.)

Prophetic Judaism

"Surely the Lord God will do nothing but he revealeth his secret unto his servants the prophets." Amos 3:7

Church of God and Saints of Christ, the congregation established as a result of the Vision Prophet William S. Crowdy received from God, observes Prophetic Judaism. Judaism is the religion based on the Hebrew Bible, a major component of which is the spirit from God that is the spirit of prophecy. A classic example of the Judaic prophetic tradition is found in the events described in II Chronicles chapter 20.

> Verse 14: Then upon Jahaziel the son of Zechariah, the son of Benaiah, the son of Jeiel, the son of Mattaniah, a Levite of the sons of Asaph, came the Spirit of the Lord in the midst of the congregation.
>
> Verse 15: And he said, Hearken ye all Judah, and ye inhabitants of Jerusalem, and thou king Jehoshaphat, Thus saith the Lord unto you, Be not afraid nor dismayed by reason of this great multitude; for the battle is not yours, but God's.

> Verse 20: And they rose early in the morning, and went forth into the wilderness of Tekoa: and as they went forth, Jehoshaphat stood and said, Hear me, O Judah, and ye inhabitants of Jerusalem; Believe in the Lord your God, so shall ye be stablished; believe his prophets; so shall ye prosper.

From the beginning, like all other faith communities that practice Judaism, the seventh day Sabbath and the Ten Commandments were paramount for the Congregation. The phrase, "The Ten Commandments," and the scripture reference of the commandments written in Exodus chapter 20 were inscribed on the seventh key of Prophet Crowdy's Vision. The interpretation later provided by Rabbi Levi S. Plummer is unconditional surrender to God. It was Rabbi Levi Plummer, with his unique eloquence, that explained Prophet Crowdy's relation to Prophetic Judaism:

> ...In the tradition of his prophetic forbearers Crowdy came forth echoing the words of Mark 1:15: "The time is fulfilled, and the kingdom of God is at hand: repent ye, and believe the

gospel." The apocalyptic urgency of His Message compelled those who heard and we who continue to listen, to act immediately.

The Divine Commission to the Prophet was deeply couched in the volume of the book and the ongoing struggle for survival of Prophetic Judaism. Out from the untamed wilderness of the Oklahoma Territory, he came forth in the "Spirit of Elijah." Confronted with an early American culture drenched in the shamefulness of slavery, existing as a lifeless valley of dry bones, he arose in the "Format of Ezekiel." With a disdain for the callous greed and selfish lust that characterize the landscape of the American political economy, he bodaciously proclaimed His Message to the rich and poor, oppressor and oppressed, Gentile and Jew, in the uncompromising "Style and Determination of Amos." [54]

Prophetic Judaism is distinct from Rabbinic Judaism, the Judaism that emerged after the destruction of the temple in Jerusalem in 70 C.E. and became what is recognized as modern Judaism in its various forms: Orthodox, Conservative, Reform and Reconstructionist. Prophetic Judaism also is distinct from what could be called biblical Judaism, when biblical is referring to both the Hebrew Bible or Old Testament and the New Testament, because the New Testament writings include groups that were not adherents of Prophetic Judaism: the Sadducees, the Pharisees, the Herodians, and the Zealots. Conventional Judaism maintains that prophecy ended with the prophets of the Hebrew Bible. A critical truth that Prophet Crowdy brought was that prophecy continued beyond the period of the Hebrew biblical prophets and that he himself was a modern exemplar of that truth.

While it was one of Prophet Crowdy's successors that labeled the faith community that he founded as adherents of Prophetic Judaism, the organization always observed the customs of Prophetic Judaism as they appear in the Bible. You will recall that Prophet Crowdy began his religious work with baptizing and washing the feet of those who chose to affiliate with him, beginning with the members of his family. [55] The Bible indicates that Jesus also practiced baptism. John

3:22 "After these things came Jesus and his disciples into the land of Judea; and there he tarried with them, and baptized." John 4:2 "Though Jesus himself baptized not, but his disciples." Madigan and Levenson say that baptism is rooted in the laws of ritual purity of the Hebrew Bible and "at some point, such immersion came to be required for those converting to Judaism..."[56] The practice of washing feet is illustrated by Jesus washing his disciples' feet as found in John chapter 13. Actually, the fourth key in Prophet Crowdy's Vision was, "Foot washing is a commandment." The accompanying scripture was St. John chapter 13 verses one through eight. The interpretation that was given to this key by Rabbi Levi S. Plummer is humility.

In addition to the rituals of baptism (now called immersion) and foot washing, in 1901 the Congregation began observing the Hebrew New Year and Passover. The New Year was observed on April 1 and the Passover on April 13.[57] The biblical reference for the New Year is Exodus chapter 12 verses one and two: "And the Lord spake unto Moses and Aaron in the land of Egypt saying, This month shall be unto you the beginning of months: it shall be the first month of the year to you."

Chief Rabbi Phillip E. McNeil, the eighth executive leader, addressed the dates for the Congregation's first and subsequent Passover Memorials in his paper, "Prophet William Saunders Crowdy is Correct: Passover Begins at Sunset Abib 13th." Rabbi McNeil writes:

> The Congregation reassembled in the hall before sunset on April 13 and proceeded to observe the Passover in a service that lasted until midnight. During the service, a leg of lamb was served family style and unleavened bread was broken and served. The meeting was adjourned until later that morning at which time a Passover day service was held on the morning of April 14.
>
> In subsequent years, when our Congregation began observing the Hebrew holy days by the Hebrew calendar, our Passover observance, in accordance with the Prophet's original instruction, was observed at sunset on Abib 13th, celebrating the Passover Memorial on the 14th day of Abib. This is in stark contrast to the widespread practice in the Jewish establishment

of observing the Passover Memorial on the 15th day of Abib. [58]

Rabbi McNeil concludes his exposition by noting that the scriptures provide for two festivals, the Passover and the Feast of Unleavened Bread.

Further, in January of 1904, Prophet Crowdy called for the observance of the fast of the tenth month referred to in Zechariah 10:19. "Thus saith the Lord of hosts; the fast of the fourth month, and the fast of the fifth, and the fast of the seventh, and the fast of the tenth, shall be to the house of Judah joy and gladness, and cheerful feasts; therefore love the truth and peace." The event is called the Holy Convocation and is observed for seven days. Prophet Crowdy also taught the Congregation to use the Hebrew names for the months of the year.

In the 1960s, during the leadership of Rabbi Howard Z. Plummer, the Congregation began using a version of the Siddur for its Beginning of Sabbath and Sabbath Day worship services. In the 1970s and 80s, during the leadership of Rabbi Levi Solomon Plummer, the Congregation began observing the other biblical holy days: Shavuoth, Rosh Hoshana, Yom Kippur, and Succoth. Since it was not until this time that the Congregation's mode of worship began to resemble that of other Jewish communities, some may conclude that prior to this period Church of God and Saints of Christ was a Christian and not Prophetic Judaism community. Particularly, given the name Church of God and Saints of Christ. That conclusion is incorrect.

First, Prophet William S. Crowdy did not have the Congregation observe any Christian holidays, such as Easter or Christmas. Second, the first century individuals who wrote the documents that became the New Testament, were themselves adherents of Prophetic Judaism. Julie Galambush's *The Reluctant Parting,* helps to illuminate this point:

> The nature, causes, and timing of the so-called parting of the ways between Judaism and Christianity are hotly debated. A few things, however, are universally agreed upon: although Jesus' first followers were Jews, mostly from Galilee, by 100 C.E. most members of the Jesus sect were Gentiles of the diaspora; by the fifth

> century "Christianity" had become a fully
> separate religion from "Judaism" (though even
> at that late date some groups resisted the split).
> Within those broad parameters, the question of
> when the Jesus movement ceased to be a Jewish
> phenomenon is nearly impossible to answer.
> Even in antiquity different people would have
> given different answers. Members of the sect
> whose ancestors were Jewish, for example,
> probably continued to see themselves as Jews far
> longer than Gentiles whose parents or
> grandparents had joined the sect when it was
> still a largely Jewish community. [59]

The religious communities that Galambush refers to as "the Jesus Movement" expressed varied interpretations of their religious faith, just like the billions of Christians in the world today reflect a diversity of denominations. These communities differed from the other first century Jewish groups because of their belief that the promise of a Messiah in the writings of the Hebrew prophets had been fulfilled in and by the life, death, and resurrection of Jesus. They were convinced that Jesus was the promised Messiah, and expected his imminent return to inaugurate the establishment of the kingdom of God. Those who could read, as most could not, were reading the Hebrew Bible or its Greek translation the Septuagint. They were worshiping on the Sabbath, as the New Testament writings attest:

> Mathew 24:20 But pray ye that your flight be not in the winter, neither on the sabbath day.
>
> Mathew 28:1 In the end of the sabbath, as it began to dawn toward the first day of the week...
>
> Mark 1:21 And they went into Capernaum; and straightway on the sabbath day he entered into the synagogue, and taught.
>
> Mark 6:2 And when the sabbath day was come, he began to teach in the synagogue...
>
> Luke 4:16 And he came to Nazareth, where he had been brought up: and, as his custom was, he went into the synagogue on the sabbath day, and stood up for to read.
>
> Luke 6:6 And it came to pass also on another sabbath, that he entered into the synagogue and taught...

Luke 10:10 And he was teaching in one of the synagogues on the sabbath.

Luke 23:54 And that day was the preparation, and the sabbath drew on.

Luke 23:56 And they returned, and prepared spices and ointments; and rested the sabbath day according to the commandment.

John 5:9 And immediately the man was made whole, and took up his bed, and walked: and on the same day was the sabbath.

Acts 13:42 And when the Jews were gone out of the synagogue, the Gentiles besought that these words might be preached to them the next sabbath.

Acts 13:44 And the next sabbath day came almost the whole city together to hear the word of God.

Acts 16:13 And on the sabbath we went out of the city by a river side, where prayer was wont to be made...

> Acts 17:2 And Paul, as his manner was, went in unto them, and three sabbath days reasoned with them out of the Scriptures.
>
> Acts 18:4 And he reasoned in the synagogue every sabbath, and persuaded the Jews and the Greeks.

Long after the first century, these groups continued to worship on the seventh day Sabbath even as pressure increased among them to distinguish themselves more conclusively from the established Judaism of their time. In fact, one writer submits that within what had become Christianity, some continued to observe the seventh day Sabbath into the fourth and fifth centuries. [60]

The New Testament writings first appeared as a proposed canon in 367 C.E. in a list prepared by Athanasius the Bishop of Alexandria, Egypt. [61] It was not until the beginning of the fifth century that these writings were universally accepted by Christians as their canon. [62] The writings were composed primarily during the first century when the authors and the communities for whom they wrote were adherents of the prophetic Judaic tradition. The Gospels reflect this:

> Mathew 5:17 Think not that I am come to destroy the law or the prophets; I am not come to destroy, but to fulfill.
>
> Mathew 10:41 He that receiveth a prophet in the name of a prophet shall receive a prophet's reward...
>
> Mathew 11:9 But what went ye out to see? A prophet? Yea, I say unto you, and more than a prophet.
>
> Mathew 14:5 And when he would have put him to death, he feared the multitude, because they counted him as a prophet.
>
> Matthew 21:11 And the multitude said, this is Jesus the prophet of Nazareth.
>
> Mark 6:4 But Jesus said unto them, A prophet is not without honor, but in his own country, and among his own kin, and in his own house.

Mark 11:32 But if we shall say, of men; they feared the people: for all men counted John, that he was a prophet indeed.

Luke 7:16 And there came a fear on all: and they glorified God, saying, That a great prophet is risen up among us; and that God hath visited his people.

Luke 7:28 For I say unto you, Among those that are born of women there is not a greater prophet than John the Baptist...

Luke 13:33 Nevertheless I must walk today and tomorrow, and the day following: for it cannot be that a prophet perish out of Jerusalem.

John 4:19 The woman saith unto him, Sir, I perceive that thou art a prophet.

John 7:40 Many of the people therefore, when they heard this saying, said, of truth this is the Prophet.

The embrace of the Hebrew biblical prophetic tradition also is present in Acts, the writings of Paul and other New Testament scriptures:

Acts 13:1 Now there were in the church that was at Antioch certain prophets and teachers...

Acts 15:32 And Judas and Silas, being prophets also themselves, exhorted the brethren with many words, and confirmed them.

Acts 21:10 And as we tarried there many days, there came down from Judea a certain prophet, named Agabus.

I Corinthians 12: 28 And God hath set some in the church, first apostles, secondarily prophets...

I Corinthians 14:29 Let the prophets speak two or three, and let the other judge.

I Corinthians 14:31 For ye may all prophesy one by one, that all may learn and all be comforted.

I Corinthians 14:32 And the spirit of the prophets are subject to the prophets.

Ephesians 4:11-12 And he gave some, apostles; and some prophets; and some, evangelists; and some, pastors and teachers; For the perfecting of the saints, for the work of the ministry, for the edifying of the body of Christ.

> Titus 1:12 One of themselves, even a prophet of their own said...
>
> Revelation 22:9 Then said he unto me, See thou do it not: for I am thy fellow servant, and of thy brethren the prophets...

The New Testament writings indicate that for these first century communities, even based upon their doctrines as they awaited the return of God's Anointed: Messiah in Hebrew; Christ in Greek, the spirit of prophecy was operative once again. To reiterate, they were Jewish believers in the presence of the prophetic spirit and not yet the new, separate Christian religion they would become over the next few centuries.

Today, it is not uncommon to hear a member of the Church of God and Saints of Christ founded by Prophet William S. Crowdy interpreting the word Christ in a way that does not equate it with the biblical Jesus. Prophet Crowdy used the language of the Bible, Old and New Testaments in his epistles, sermons, and the publication "set forth" by him, *The Revelation of God Revealed*. It does appear that when he used the word Christ, he was referring to Jesus. Yet, just like the New Testament writers, he made an absolute distinction between God and Jesus, and he did not teach that Jesus was God.

It was Rabbi Levi S. Plummer, who explicitly articulated the organization's doctrine as believing that Jesus was a prophet but not the Messiah. Indeed, the Church of God and Saints of Christ does not believe in the concept of a future individual Messiah, but in a future "Messianic Age." If there is a difference on this issue between the Congregation's doctrine today and the days of Prophet Crowdy, this is fully consistent with his prophetic decree, that there were men coming behind him who would clarify and refine the way of life that he only was able to give in chunks. As the prophet Hosea wrote, "And by a prophet the Lord brought Israel out of Egypt, and by a prophet was he preserved." And by a prophet, William S. Crowdy, God created the community of faith that is Church of God and Saints of Christ, Temple Beth El, International Headquarters, and by a prophet is it preserved.[63]

Epilogue

Throughout history there have been men and women who used their personal encounters with the Divine to form communities to assist others with their spiritual lives. Prophet William S. Crowdy was one of those individuals. When he was sixteen, he fled from the plantation where he was born. Unbeknown to him, he would spend the last sixteen years of his life as a Divinely selected servant of God. He died seven days before his sixty-first birthday. One of his prayers was that his biological descendants would be actively involved in the Congregation that he started. His great grandson served as the seventh executive leader, and members of his family remain active participants in the way of life that he re-established.

Bibliography

Collier-Thomas, Bettye, *Daughters of Thunder,* San Francisco: Jossey-Bass, 1998.

Copher, Charles B., "The Black Presence in the Old Testament," Cain Hope Felder, ed. *Stony The Road We Trod,* Minneapolis: Fortress Press, 1991.

Ehrman, Bart D., *The New Testament: A Historical Introduction to the Early Christian Writings, 5th Ed.,* New York: Oxford University Press, 2012.

Felder, Cain Hope, ed., *The Original African Heritage Study Bible,* Nashville: James C. Winston Publishing Company, 1993.

Felder, Cain Hope, *Race, Racism, and the Biblical Narratives,* Minneapolis: Fortress Press, 2002.

Galambush, Julie, *The Reluctant Parting,* New York: HarperCollins Press, 2005.

Madigan, Kevin J. and Jon D. Levenson, *Resurrection,* New Haven: Yale University Press, 2008.

Masequesmay, G., "Sexism," Encyclopedia Britannica, 2014.

McDonald, Kelly, Jr., "Sabbath Keeping in the 300s-400s AD," *The Sabbath Sentinel,* June 28, 2019.

McNeil, Phillip E., "Prophet William S. Crowdy is Correct: Passover Begins at Sundown on Abib 13th," unpublished paper, 2020.

Metzger, Bruce M. and Michael D. Coogan, eds, *The Oxford Essential Guide to Ideas & Issues of the Bible,* New York: Berkley Books, 2002.

Moscati, Sabatino, *The Face of the Ancient Orient,* Mineola: Dover Publications, Inc., 2001.

Nadell, Pamela S., *Women Who Would Be Rabbis,* Boston: Beacon Press, 1998.

Nash, Peter T. *Reading Race, Reading the Bible,* Minneapolis: Augsburg Fortress, 2003, Nook.

Selected Sermons and Epistles of Prophet William S. Crowdy and Other Related Materials, Belleville: Church of God and Saints of Christ, 1981.

Sernett, Milton C., *African American Religious History, A Documentary Witness*, 2d ed., Durham: Duke University Press, 1999.

Shimron, Yonat, Washington Post, November 13, 2020.

Sweet Songs of Zion: Official Hymnal of Church of God and Saints of Christ, Suffolk: Union Choir, 2017.

The History of the Church of God and Saints of Christ Volume II (1908 – 1996), Suffolk: Church of God and Saints of Christ, 1996

The Re-Establishing Years: History of Church of God and Saints of Christ, Suffolk: Church of God and Saints of Christ, 1992.

Walker, Beersheba Crowdy, *Life and Works of William Saunders Crowdy,* Philadelphia: Elfreth J. P. Walker, 1955.

Notes

[1] Beersheba Crowdy Walker, *Life and Works of William Saunders Crowdy* (Philadelphia: Elfreth J. P. Walker, 1955), 2.

[2] *The Re-Establishing Years: History of the Church of God and Saints of Christ* (Suffolk: Church of God and Saints of Christ, 1992), 11-12.

[3] Ibid, 20-22.

[4] Walker, *Life and Works of William Saunders Crowdy*, 8-9.

[5] Ibid, 14-15.

[6] *The Re-Establishing Years, 47-48*.

[7] Ibid, 50; *The History of the Church of God and Saints of Christ Volume II (1908 – 1996)* (Suffolk: Church of God and Saints of Christ, 1996), 39.

[8] Walker, *Life and Works of William Saunders Crowdy*, 44.

[9] *The Re-Establishing Years,* 50.

[10] *The History of the Church of God and Saints of Christ Volume II (1908 -1996), 39-40.*

[11] Ibid, 40.

[12] Walker, *Life and Works of William Saunders Crowdy*, 11-12.

[13] *The Re-Establishing Years,* 28-31.

[14] Ibid, 68.

[15] *Selected Sermons and Epistles of Prophet William S. Crowdy and Other Related Materials* (Belleville: Church of God and Saints of Christ, 1981), 63.

[16] Walker, *Life and Works of William Saunders Crowdy*, 12.

[17] Milton C. Sernett, *African American Religious History, A Documentary Witness*, 2d ed. (Durham: Duke University Press, 1999), 465. The Pentecostal Assemblies of the World founded in 1908 also was inter-racial.

[18] Yonat Shimron, Washington Post, November 13, 2020.

[19] Walker, *Life and Works of William Saunders Crowdy*, 11; *Selected Sermons and Epistles of Prophet William S. Crowdy and Other Related Materials*, 3-13.

[20] Charles B. Copher, "The Black Presence in the Old Testament," Cain Hope Felder, ed., *Stony the Road We Trod* (Minneapolis: Fortress Press, 1991), 150-151.

[21] Cain Hope Felder, *Race, Racism, and the Biblical Narratives* (Minneapolis: Fortress Press, 2002), 3.

[22] Peter T. Nash, *Reading Race, Reading the Bible* (Minneapolis: Augsburg Fortress, 2003), 32, Nook.

[23] Daniel C. Snell, *Religions of the Ancient Near East* (New York: Cambridge University Press, 2011), 2.

[24] Sabatino Moscati, *The Face of the Ancient Orient* (Mineola: Dover Publications, Inc., 2001), 19.

[25] John G. Jackson, *Man, God, and Civilization* (Chicago: Lushena Books, 2000), 242.

[26] Ibid, *188*.

[27] Copher, "The Black Presence in the Old Testament," 154.

[28] The Reverend Cain Hope Felder, Ph.D., ed., *The Original African Heritage Study Bible* (Nashville: The James C. Winston Publishing Company, 1993), xiv-xv.

[29] Ibid.

[30] Pamela S. Nadell, *Women Who Would Be Rabbis* (Boston: Beacon Press, 1998) 1.

[31] Walker, *Life and Works of William Saunders Crowdy*, 23.

[32] Ibid. 42.

[33] Ibid, 49.

[34] Ibid, 42.

[35] In the biographical statement included in the Centennial Commemorative Journal of the congregation Evangelist Malinda Morris started it states that she received ministerial credentials at the Annual Assembly in Philadelphia.

[36] Walker, *Life and Works of William Saunders Crowdy*, 42.

[37] Ibid, 44.

[38] Ibid, 57.

[39] Ibid, 60. (In the Centennial Commemorative Journal of her organization it says, that Evangelist Morris was out of the pulpit for one year and that from Washington, DC, Prophet William S. Crowdy sent for her, restored her to the pulpit and

told her, "go back to your pulpit and stay there until Christ comes."

40 *Selected Sermons and Epistles of Prophet William S. Crowdy and Other Related Materials, 50, 55.*
41 *The Re-Establishing Years,* 68.
42 Walker, *Life and Works of William Saunders Crowdy,* 11.
43 Ibid, 11-12.
44 Ibid. 54.
45 Masequesmay, G. "Sexism." Encyclopedia Britannica, 2014. https://www.britannica.com/topic/sexism.
46 Bettye Collier-Thomas, *Daughters of Thunder* (San Francisco: Jossey-Bass, 1998), xiv.
47 Walker, *Life and Works of William Saunders Crowdy,* 45.
48 *Selected Sermons and Epistles of Prophet William S. Crowdy and Other Related Materials,* 21.
49 Ibid, 50.
50 Collier-Thomas, *Daughters of Thunder,* 18.
51 Walker, *Life and Works of William Saunders Crowdy,* 57.
52 *Selected Sermons and Epistles of Prophet William S. Crowdy and Other Related Materials,* 26.
53 Ibid, 40.
54 *The Re-Establishing Years,* v.
55 Walker, *Life and Works of William Saunders Crowdy,* 9.
56 Kevin J. Madigan and Jon D. Levenson, *Resurrection* (New Haven: Yale University Pres, 2008), 10.
57 *The Re-Establishing Years,* 43.
58 Chief Rabbi Phillip E. McNeil, "Prophet William Saunders Crowdy is Correct: Passover Begins at Sunset on Abib 13th," unpublished paper, March 9, 2020.
59 Julie Galambush, *The Reluctant Parting* (New York: HarperCollins Press, 2005), 15-16.
60 Kelly McDonald, Jr., "Sabbath Keeping in the 300s-400s AD," The Sabbath Sentinel, June 28, 2019.
61 Bart D. Ehrman, *The New Testament: A Historical Introduction to the Early Christian Writings, 5th Ed.,* 11.

[62] Bruce M. Metzger and Michael D. Coogan, eds, *The Oxford Essential Guide to Ideas & Issues of the Bible* (New York: Berkley Books, 2002), 86.
[63] *Sweet Songs of Zion: Official Hymnal of Church of God and Saints of Christ,* (Suffolk: Union Choir, 2017), 193.

www.ingramcontent.com/pod-product-compliance
Lightning Source LLC
LaVergne TN
LVHW051710080426
835511LV00017B/2837